Rain Stops Play

Rain Stops Play

Brian Johnston

with cartoons by
Bill Tidy

Edited by
Lynn Hughes

W. H. Allen · London
A Howard & Wyndham Company
1979

Published August 1979 by
W. H. Allen & Co. Ltd,
44 Hill Street, London W1X 8LB

Printed and bound in Great Britain
by W & J Mackay Limited, Chatham

ISBN 0 491 02328 6

Dedication

To: Rlow, Arl, Blowers, Boilers, Sir Frederick, The Alderman, Jenkers, The Bearded Wonder and Backers—With grateful thanks for the way in which they have tolerated my jokes (?) and antics in the Box.

Contents

Contents

Introduction

When people ask me where I work, I sometimes reply: 'In a box'. Actually I don't *really* work, anyway. I just go to a match with some friends who love cricket as much as I do. Together we try to tell hundreds of thousands of other cricket lovers about the game which we are watching. We are an extrovert lot and completely different in character. And yet, in all my thirty-three years of commentating, I have never had a row with anyone in the Box.

There's a relaxed, friendly atmosphere which often seems to surprise visitors who come to see how we work. They expect to find nervous tension and suspense. Instead there is a kind of disorganised calm plus, I must admit, a certain amount of schoolboy humour. This is partly explained by the fact that we all think that cricket is fun. So we *have* fun. We are delighted to know that some of this manages to come through the microphone into people's homes, cars or wherever they may be listening. We know that some have a small transistor hidden in their office drawers. There are others who work in factories or shops and walk around with a pocket radio and ear-plugs. If asked to explain, they admit to being a little deaf! Many thousands also check up on us by watching TV and listening to *our* radio commentary. And of course many spectators in the crowd at a Test Match listen at the same time to Test Match Special.

Judging by the hundreds of letters which come pouring in during the Tests our listeners are of all ages and types and listen for many different reasons. Some are cricket mad like us and want to know exactly what happens to every ball. Others keep their own scorebooks or check up on the records to see if they can catch Bill Frindall out. Many people, such as doctors and commercial travellers, listen in their cars between appointments. And last, but by no means least, come the ladies who keep us as a background to their housework and cooking.

It is because we know that we have this enthusiastic and apparently appreciative band of faithful followers, that we try to do our best never to return to the studio for music when play is interrupted for some reason or other. During long periods of rain we chat away amongst ourselves or invite old cricketers or personalities in other walks of life to join us in the Box. Naturally we try to stick mostly to cricket, answering queries sent in by letter, reminiscing or even trying to catch each other out with quiz questions. It really does become a chat show and many people—especially the ladies—have told me that they think it far better when it is raining than when cricket is being played!

I think that all of us in the Test Match Special Team have at some time written a book or even books. But it was suggested to me that it might be fun to collect *under one heading* some of the amusing incidents which have happened to us in the Box. There are the gaffes made by TV and radio commentators during actual commentary, the leg-pulls and funny happenings which have taken place behind the scenes, and the cricket stories which have been told during our conversations when Rain Stops Play.

Now, for the first time, the stories are illustrated with the supreme artistic touch of someone who is another cricket fanatic—cartoonist Bill Tidy. He also thinks that cricket is fun. So we hope that our combined efforts will give everyone who loves cricket a few laughs, and cheer them up on this sticky wicket of a world in which we now live.

Slips

We start with some of the gaffes, slips of the tongue or innuendos which have been made on radio or TV over the last thirty years or so. As the chief gaffer myself, I can only assure you that I never do them on purpose and that all of them are perfectly genuine. Funnily enough, although some of them may appear rather rude, no one ever seems to write in and complain. This may be due to the fact that we have all been taught never to stop and apologise. Just go straight on and the listener won't believe that he or she has heard aright!

1974 at Old Trafford—England v India. It was raining heavily on Saturday morning. The covers were on, everyone with umbrellas or macintoshes, the Indian spectators sitting huddled up looking miserable and cold. Test Match Special came over to me at 11.25—Any chance of any play Brian?' 'No, I'm afraid not,' I said, 'it's raining hard, it's cold and miserable, the covers are still on. It doesn't look as if it will get any better either . . .' (and here I *meant* to say, 'There's a dirty black cloud') . . . *'There's a dirty black crowd here!'*

At Northampton in 1976 Northants were playing Worcestershire at Northampton where spectators can drive their cars in and sit in them to watch the play around the ground. It was quite an important match as Northants were in with a chance of drawing level with Middlesex at the head of the County Championship table. In spite of this there was a disappointingly small crowd. So I said, to introduce the game, 'There's a small crowd here to watch this important game—*in fact I would say that there are more cars here than people!*'

At Trent Bridge in 1950—England v West Indies—Worrell and Weekes put on 283 for 4th wicket for West Indies and on the Friday evening were hitting the English bowling all over the field. We got a bit tired of showing four after four so to vary things I said, 'I wonder what Norman Yardley (England's Captain) is going to do to separate the two batsmen.' The camera obediently panned round to Weekes at mid-on but unfortunately he was scratching himself in a very awkward place! To cover up this I had to say something quickly and came out with '*Obviously a very ticklish problem*'.

At Leicester two years ago I am told I welcomed listeners with 'You've come over at a very appropriate time *Ray Illingworth has just relieved himself at the pavilion end.*'

On one occasion I said that Freddie Titmus was bowling and that he had *two short legs—one of them square*. A listener wrote in to say that he was travelling in a car in Belgium listening to our commentary, and trying to explain cricket to two Belgian friends. When the Belgian lady heard my remark she asked why it was necessary to draw attention to a player's physical disabilities!

3

At Hove in a match between Sussex and Hampshire, Henry Horton of Hampshire was batting and I thought I should tell the radio listeners about his funny stance at the

wicket—he stuck his bottom out in a most peculiar way. So I *meant* to say 'Henry Horton has got a funny sort of stance—it looks as if he's sitting on a shooting stick' —BUT I got it the wrong way round!

At Lord's in 1969. England v New Zealand. Ward is bowling very fast from the pavilion end to Glenn Turner.

Off the fifth ball of one of his overs he hit Turner a terrible blow in the box. Turner collapses, bat going one way, his gloves another. TV Camera pans in. I have to pretend he's been hit everywhere except where he has been! (*Nowadays* one *would* say!) Turner writhes in pain in the crease for a minute or so, then slowly gets to his feet. Someone hands him his bat, someone else his gloves. I say, '*Turner looks a bit shaky and unsteady but I think he's going to bat on—one ball left.*'

At Worcester on one occasion I greeted the listeners with 'Welcome to Worcester *where you've just missed seeing Barry Richards hitting one of Basil D'Oliveira's balls clean out of the ground.*'

I was at Southampton one Saturday to commentate on a match between Hampshire and Surrey. Rex Alston was up at Edgbaston for a Warwickshire match. At Southampton they started at 11.30 a.m. and finished at 6.30 p.m. But at Edgbaston they did not start till 12 noon, so play was due to end at 7 p.m. At close of play at Southampton I wrapped up saying we had had a good day, etc. and that at close of play the score was such and such. I went on to explain that the listeners could still hear some more commentary as play went on at Edgbaston for another half an hour. So I said 'Goodbye from Southampton *and over now to Edgbaston for some more balls from Rex Alston.*'

On another occasion Ken Barington had made a hundred and I said that he was playing well now, but was a bit lucky, as he was *dropped when two*. Believe it or not a letter came in from a listener complaining about the carelessness of mothers!

6

Roy Lawrence during the 3rd test West Indies v England at Sabina Park in 1960. '*It's another wonderful day here at Sabina Park—the wind shining and the sun blowing gently across the field.*'

Rex also is reputed to have said: '*Over now to Old John Arlott at Trafford*'.

At the Oval in 1976 England were playing the West Indies and after the match a lady wrote to me saying how much she had enjoyed our commentaries but that I ought to be

more careful, as we had a lot of young listeners. She asked if I realised what I said when they came to me as Michael Holding was bowling to Peter Willey. She told me that I had said: *'The bowler's holding the batsman's willy.'*

I MAKE IT 111·5 ACTUALLY!

John Snagge was once reading the latest cricket scores. He said: 'Yorkshire 232 all out—*Hutton ill—no I'm sorry —Hutton 111.'*

I was once doing a commentary on the annual Whitsun match between Middlesex and Sussex when John Warr was captain of Middlesex. Middlesex were batting and making a big score when I had to hand back to the studio for another programme. After a while they handed back to me at Lord's for the latest news and I began, 'Well the latest news here is that *Warr's declared*.' The duty officer at the time in Broadcasting House told me later that an old lady had switched on as I said this and rang up the duty officer to see whom it was against!

At Headingley in 1961—England v Australia, Australians fielding. Camera pans in unexpectedly on Neil Harvey. B.J. having to say something quickly. '*There's Neil Harvey standing at leg slip with his legs wide apart waiting for a tickle.*'

One unknown commentator is reputed to have said: '*He was bowled by a ball which he should have left alone!*'

Robert Hudson during England v New Zealand at Lord's in 1969. The two teams are being presented to the Queen and Prince Philip during the tea interval . . . *'It's obviously a great occasion for all of them. It's a moment they will always forget.'*

Surprisingly I have never heard John Arlott make a gaffe. So let's reward him by printing one of the best of his many *bon mots*. He was describing the Pakistan fast bowler Asif Masood's action. You may remember that he used to run up with bent knees. John described him perfectly: 'He reminds me,' he said, 'of Groucho Marx chasing a pretty waitress!'

At Lords during a Middlesex match Rex Alston once said, *'No runs from that over bowled by Jack Young, which means that he has now had 4 maidens on the trot!'*

Rex also once said that one of the Captains had asked for *'the medium pace roller'*.

Another commentator on England's tour of Australia in 1978/79 said: 'John Emburey is bowling with three short legs—*one of them wearing a helmet!'*

On air: Vision on

In 1946 and 1947 my fellow TV commentators included Percy Fender and R. C. (Crusoe) Robertson-Glasgow. We all had to learn to take the producer's instructions in our head-phones at the same time as giving a commentary—we also had to take care not to answer him back into the microphone. Crusoe had once just given the score in some detail when he heard the producer say: 'I think it's about time to give the score Crusoe.' Crusoe just managed not to say something like 'I've just given it you bloody fool!' Instead he said into the microphone: 'For those of you who were not paying attention when I gave the score just now, here it is again.'

Percy Fender had a rather quiet, confidential voice and on one occasion the sound engineer from the control scanner asked him to speak up a bit. I looked across and saw that Percy was holding the 'lip' microphone some way from his mouth, whereas it should be held right up against it. The engineer obviously realised this because he went on to say, 'Hold the mike closer so that it's touching the end of your nose.' Percy whispered to me angrily: '*I am* doing so.' And he was right—he was. But his nose was nearly as long as mine so that the mike was still too far away from his mouth.

Once I was commentating for Radio on a County Match at Clacton on Sea. Essex were fielding and Trevor Bailey—unusually for him—had placed himself in the deep. One or two balls came to him and although he stopped them he didn't look too lively. Finally he did let one through for a boundary and I commented that he didn't look too energetic and possibly he had had too good a party the night before. As I said it I was watching him and he turned round to my commentary box and shook his fist at me! I hadn't realised that he could hear my commentary from a portable radio belonging to someone sitting in a deckchair on the boundary. A salutary lesson to be careful what one says over the air!

On the 31st December 1958 I made my very first Test Commentary in Australia. It was during Peter May's tour of 1958/59 and England having lost the 1st Test at Brisbane were 7 for 3 in their 1st innings of the 2nd Test when

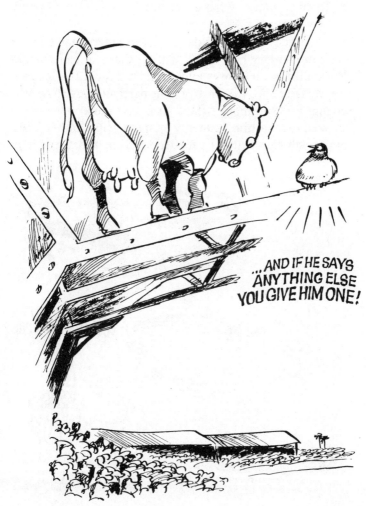

I started my first commentary. I had only said a few words about how pleased I was to be working for ABC when I felt a splash on my wrist. It was a pigeon which had dropped a message of welcome from one of the steel rafters of the vast Melbourne stand. What a welcome!

One Saturday Robert Hudson was the commentator in our old commentary box in the Warner Stand at Lord's. Bill Frindall was the scorer and Freddie Brown the 'expert' summariser. At the end of one particular over he was giving his summary when listeners must have been amazed to hear him suddenly let out a yelp—rather like a puppy which has had its toe trodden on. What had hap-

pened was this. Robert was always a tremendous fiddler whilst commentating. He used his hands the whole time to pick up pencils or rubbers, bits of paper or books, etc. In those days Bill used to secure his score sheets to wooden boards with large rubber bands. These were special favourites of Robert's who used to pull them out and stretch them to their utmost limits. He had just finished describing a particularly exciting over, during which he had been fiddling away with one of the rubber bands. As Freddie started his summary Robert fiddled once too often, and one of the bands came off the board. As if catapulted it shot across the box and hit Freddie a stinging blow in the left ear. But apart from the yelp—a natural reaction—and a nervous glance over his left shoulder, Freddie continued talking, not sure whether he had been stung by a wasp or struck by a poisoned dart! It is not surprising that during his MCC tour of Australia in 1950–51 they said that Freddie Brown had a heart the size of October cabbages.

I have this habit of sometimes addressing my colleagues in the box as Sir—especially Freddie Trueman whom I often address as Sir Frederick. When my last book—*It's a funny game*—came out I sent off copies to all the commentators and cricket writers. I wrote something in each one, and my publishers, W. H. Allen, then posted them off for me. In Freddie's I put something like: 'To Sir Frederick With happy memories of days together in the commentary box . . .'

I thought no more about it until I heard from Don Mosey that Fred was very annoyed with me. Evidently his friend the regular postman came rushing up the path one

morning shouting, 'Congratulations Freddie—you've got it at last—you've got it.' He handed a surprised Fred a parcel obviously containing a book and addressed to
        Sir Frederick Trueman!
Later I discovered what had happened. The girl who dispatched all the books from W. H. Allen had looked inside the book and seeing my message to 'Sir Frederick' really thought he *was* a Knight!

Once when televising at Lord's I noticed John Warr sitting with his fiancée Valerie in the Grandstand. We quickly got the cameras on to them and introduced them to the viewing public as Warr and Piece.

One incident in 1953 which concerned Jim Swanton still remains a mystery to this day. Jim was commentating on TV at the Headingley Test v Australia when a man walked past our commentary point. He was carrying a ladder over his shoulder and round his neck—like a giant collar—was a lavatory seat. As you can imagine, he caused quite a commotion in the crowd, as he disappeared under the football stand. But Jim with his usual *sang-froid* (and good taste!) completely ignored the man, even though he had been picked up by our cameras. Instead, Jim drew the viewers' attention to Lindwall's beautiful action out in the middle.

Almost ten minutes later the man reappeared from under the stand and walked back past our commentary box still with the ladder *but minus the seat*. What *had* he done with it; and if he had had to fix it, why did he need a ladder? Jim again ignored him and offered no solution to this mysterious happening. I only wished that I had been

19

doing the commentary at the time! But perhaps it is just as well that I wasn't.

In the summer of 1978 at the Oval I registered a 'first' in the radio commentary box. We had two policemen up on our balcony at the top of the pavilion, and as it was a hot day they took off their helmets. As I was commentating, someone—I'm not sure who—took one of the helmets and

"YOU'LL JUST HAVE TO HOPE HE DOESN'T NOTICE!"

put it on my head. I now have a certificate to register that I am the first BBC commentator to give a live cricket commentary wearing a policeman's helmet—belonging to PC 418 Barry Brown.

One amusing incident which happened to Jim Swanton, which was *not* a leg-pull, though at the time he was suspicious that we had organised it. At the end of each day of a Test Match, Jim used to appear in vision and give one of his superb summaries of the day's play. On one occasion at Trent Bridge he was giving his summary in vision from our television platform above the balcony of the pavilion. He always, for some reason, used to have his field glasses slung round his neck. At the end of this particular summary he said: 'Well, there it is then. A really good day's cricket. One, I think, which we will always remember. So as I say goodnight, I'll just repeat the close of play score for you . . .' As he said this he removed his field glasses from around his neck and placed them on the small table in front of him. He then looked up at the giant electric scoreboard to read out the score but to his horror, saw that it was completely blank. Everything had been switched off! As sometimes happens to most of us, his mind, too, went blank and he couldn't remember the final score. With a muttered apology he snapped his fingers and one of the TV assistants quickly wrote him the score on a piece of paper for him to read out. But it was a nasty moment!

In the Box

The expert is a vital ingredient to a cricket commentary team.
He is almost always an ex-Test player who can interpret the
finer points of the game because he has been out in the middle
himself. On television nowadays ex-Test players provide both
the commentary and the summaries. On radio the commentary
is almost always done by broadcasters and the summaries by
ex-Test players. Their guidance and expertise make our job so
much easier and we value their presence in the Box more than
we can say. But that does not mean that they are not human
like the rest of us—as one or two of these stories will show. . . .

On the Saturday of the Oval Test between England and
Australia in 1977 we all got a shock when we first entered
the commentary box before play started. There, sitting in
Bill Frindall's usual corner, was an Arab in full white Arab
dress and head-dress. He was a bearded figure who kept
his head down, apparently absorbed in Bill's score sheets
and record books. We none of us knew what to do except
to mutter Good Morning to which the Arab murmured
something into his beard without looking up. We, of
course, suspected it might be a leg-pull, but on the other
hand it could be someone from the BBC Arab Service,
who was to be attached to us for the day. Anyhow, none of
us dared to be the first to challenge the stranger. However,

just before we went on the air it became obvious that it must be Bill Frindall, since he had not yet appeared in the box—at least as himself. On being challenged he pleaded guilty, but it was still difficult to believe that it was not a genuine Arab, with Bill's big black beard and authentic white Arab dress. All that was missing was a camel tied up outside the box!

During the morning we explained to listeners what had happened and questioned him about it. Evidently the night before he had been at a party and had been introduced to an Arab in Arab dress. This Arab thought that Bill was also an Arab—from his dark, swarthy appearance—and started to speak to him in Arabic. Bill's hostess hurriedly explained the mistake, but there and then bet Bill that he would not spend a whole day at the Oval Test dressed as an Arab. Her Arab friend promised to lend his clothes and so Bill said he would do it for charity. Sponsorship for £62 was soon guaranteed, the proceeds to go to Cancer Research if Bill succeeded.

Next morning when he drove his car up to the Oval gates the attendant was surprised to see an Arab driving a car with the Official Car Park label stuck on the windscreen. However, he let the car through and Bill immediately drove to the usual space which was always reserved for him near the back door to the pavilion. Another worried official ran up: 'Hey, you can't park there. It's always reserved for Mr Bill Frindall as he has so many brief-cases to carry.' Bill muttered through his beard that he couldn't care less for Mr Frindall. 'I have just bought up the Oval,' he said, 'and I shall park where I like.' Then, to spare the astonished official—an old friend—any more embarrassment, Bill revealed who he was. He made his way through the crowd in the pavilion

'LOTS OF SPONSORSHIP TODAY!'

up to the commentary box. He somehow managed to keep a straight face as we all muttered our tentative greetings.

He stayed in his Arab dress all day and so won his bet for charity. The white robes, he told us on the air, were called *Dish Dash* and had once belonged to King Hussein, who had given them away to a friend. 'I don't blame him,' said Fred Trueman, 'I would have done the same thing to get rid of them!'

Once, when I was commentating for radio at a match at Leyton, Peter Cranmer, who was at Worcester, overran his allotted time. However, he eventually handed over to me and I couldn't resist greeting him with: 'Better Leyton than never.'

Nowadays television commentary boxes are far more accessible than they were when we first started. They used to be on a high platform supported by scaffolding, and could only be reached by climbing an ordinary builders' ladder. This was terrifying for the likes of me who are scared of heights. But it also used to produce some good laughs for the crowds. I remember well the barracking and shouts of encouragement which they used to give to Roy Webber and Jim Swanton—at that time the bulkiest of the commentators—as they made their perilous climbs. Actually on a windy day, when the scaffolding swayed dangerously, we were very pleased to have them with us up there as ballast. Once at the Oval the crowd had an extra bonus so far as ladder-climbing entertainment went. The cameramen, riggers and sound engineers used to come up to our balcony on top of the pavilion via an iron ladder fixed against a stone wall. It was a short cut and saved them going through the pavilion. At one Test Match a *very* high BBC executive had lunched somewhere rather well with a lady. After lunch they decided they would like to watch the Test at the Oval. The executive had no ticket to the pavilion but paid at the gates to gain admittance to the ground. He walked round to where the TV scanners were parked and saw some of the TV crew climing the iron ladder up to our commentary position on the balcony. So he decided that he in his black homburg, and his lady friend—who was dressed in a thin summer dress and wearing a big picture hat—should follow them. They started their climb amidst roars of laughter and shouts of encouragement from the members in the stand at the side of the pavilion. The ladder went up a long way above this stand and as the intrepid climbers slowly passed the members, there were loud gasps from the men, and some

squeals of delight from the ladies. What the executive had
not realised was that there was a strong wind blowing and
that the skirt of his lady friend who was following him up
the ladder, was billowing around her neck revealing (luck-
ily!) a pair of very snazzy knickers!

On one occasion Tony Brown of Gloucestershire went off
the field and we were told that he had a very poisoned toe
and that he had to take his boot off as his toe was oozing
pus (ugh!). 'What pantomime does that remind you of?' I
asked my colleagues. Getting no reply I told them: 'Pus(s)
in Boots'.

At the end of the 4th Test v Australia at the Oval in 1975, Trevor Bailey was discussing whether England should have taken more risks in their 2nd innings and how by scoring more quickly, they might have won the match. '. . . if they had taken risks of course, there was always the danger of them losing quick wickets. It's very difficult to know how to strike a happy medium.' I couldn't resist interrupting: 'You *could* go to a seance'—amidst the rightful groans from the others in the box.

On another hot day—this time at Headingley—Arthur Gilligan was the summariser. After lunch he fell asleep and as he dozed he vaguely heard Rex Alston's voice droning on without taking in what he was saying. Suddenly Arthur woke with a start as Rex nudged him and said, 'That's how I saw the incident—what do *you* say, Arthur?' Arthur reacted quickly for one who had only just woken up. 'I entirely agree with everything you have just said, Rex—I couldn't have put it better myself . . .' he replied as his chin sunk once more onto his chest.

During the Summer of 1971 Pakistan and India were the joint tourists. Throughout the Indian Test Matches whenever the Indian wicket-keeper let through a bye or byes off Bishen Bedi, we couldn't resist calling them 'Bedi byes'.

Pulls to Leg

Earlier on I stressed that the atmosphere in the Box is friendly, relaxed and spiced with a certain amount of schoolboy humour. Here now are some of the leg-pulls which we have perpetrated from time to time on an unsuspecting colleague.

At Port of Spain during Colin Cowdrey's successful MCC Tour in 1967, I played a dirty trick on Tony Cozier. Rain had stopped play and he had gone across to the press box on the other side of the ground. I stayed in the box to give an occasional up to date report on the weather. I saw him returning after a time, so as he entered the box I pretended that we were on the air, and that I was broadcasting. 'Well, I began, those were the statistics of the MCC Team with their exact batting and bowling figures, plus their ages and dates of their birthdays. Ah, I see that Tony Cozier has just rejoined us, so I will ask him to give exactly the same details of the whole West Indian side. Tony . . . ' I have rarely seen a greater look of horror on anyone's face. He sat down at the mike and began to stammer, making frantic signals to our scorer to hand him Wisden or any other book which would give him the necessary information. 'Well, Brian,' he said, 'I'll try to tell the listeners in a minute, but as I've just seen the pitch perhaps you would like to hear about its state first.' 'No, sorry, Tony.' I

said—'we've just talked about it whilst you were away. All we want—and straight away please—is the information about the West Indian Statistics.' At this point I couldn't go on any further, he looked so miserable and desperate, so I said: 'Well, if Tony won't give us the details I suppose we had better return to the studio.' There was a deathly hush for about five seconds and then I broke the news to him that we had *not* been on the air! It took him quite a time to get over the shock, and I sometimes wonder if he has ever forgiven me!

For many years Jim Swanton, Peter West, Denis Compton and I did the television commentaries and we found that Jim was a perfect target for leg-pulls. Here are a few:

At Lords in 1963 we were televising that magnificent Test Match between England and the West Indies which ended in such an exciting draw. On the Friday, while we were commentating, the Sacred College of Cardinals were in conclave in the Vatican to elect a new Pope to succeed the late Pope John XXIII. The crowds were assembled in St Peter's Square awaiting the puff of white smoke to come from the chimney in the Vatican which would announce that a new Pope had been elected. I suddenly spotted that one of the chimneys in the old tavern had caught fire and that black smoke was belching out of it. With the help of producer Antony Craxton the cameras were quickly directed onto it and I was able to say, 'Ah, I see that Jim Swanton has been elected Pope!'

In 1964 for some reason Jim had a chauffeur to drive him round the various matches which he was covering. On the first morning of the 1st Test Match v Australia at Trent

Bridge Jim was as usual one of the commentators on TV. At about 12 noon Denis Compton slipped out of the box and took down a message to the man on the public address. We had composed this up in the box when Jim wasn't looking and during a silence between overs the loudspeakers boomed out to the packed crowd: 'If Mr E. W. Swanton has arrived on the ground yet will he please go at once to the back of the pavilion where his chauffeur has left the engine of his car running.' I have rarely heard such laughter on a cricket ground, and Jim of course soon knew where to put the blame.

In 1963 we were televising the August Bank Holiday match between Kent and Hampshire at Canterbury. Jim was one of the commentators and Colin Cowdrey was in our box as an expert after breaking his wrist in the Lord's Test. Before play we got together with that arch leg-puller Peter Richardson, who was Captain of Kent, and Bill Copson, one of the umpires. Kent were batting and we laid our plans which were to start as soon as a handkerchief was waved from our TV box as a signal that Jim Swanton was commentating. As soon as he saw the signal, Peter—who was one of the batsmen—had an earnest mid-wicket conference with his partner, ostentatiously gesticulating in our direction. He then went over to Copson and spoke gravely to him, still pointing to us. Antony Craxton zoomed one of his cameras in on the pitch and said to him, 'I wonder what's going on? What's the conference all about? Comment on it please.' At this point Copson began walking towards our commentary box. 'Ah,' said Jim, 'obviously some small boys are playing about below us here and putting the batsmen off—or perhaps its the sun shining on the windscreen of a car . . .' Copson stopped when twenty yards short of our box,

34

cupped his hands and shouted so that the millions of viewers could hear: 'Will you stop that booming noise up there. It's putting the batsmen off. Please stop it.' Colin, just to rub it in, pretended not to have heard and shouted down to Copson: 'Sorry, can you repeat that?' Copson did so, twice as loud, and there was a roar of laughter from the crowd, and Jim soon realised that his leg had been well and truly pulled.

Rex Alston was commentating at Lord's with Jim Swanton as his summariser. Rex tended to hold his head between his hands when broadcasting—so that he looked

COMMENTATORS
BOX

straight ahead—rather like a horse in blinkers. A batsman snicked a ball which fell just in front of 2nd slip. 'I don't think that was a chance but as it's the end of the over, let's ask Jim Swanton what *he* thought.' He turned round, and to his horror found an empty seat beside him and on the desk a short note which read: 'Have gone to spend a penny. Back in a minute. Jim.'

On one hot sticky day during Mike Smith's MCC tour of South Africa in 1965 I was in the commentary box at Johannesburg with Charles Fortune. At the end of my commentary spell I handed over to Charles who had just slipped into the seat beside me. I was amazed to see that he was sitting there in his underpants, with his trousers hanging up on a peg—the first time I had experienced a fellow commentator literally revealing the bare facts.

With one exception I have very happy memories of commentating on any match in which India has been playing. The exception was one Sunday in 1967 when India was playing Lancashire at Southport in a 40-over-a-side game. I was working for television but instead of commentating I was doing in-vision interviews with the batsmen as they returned to the pavilion. It's not a particularly easy job as most batsmen are not in a very good mood after being dismissed—especially as nowadays no one ever seems to think that they are out.

I was sitting with my microphone in a deck-chair in front of the pavilion when I saw that Wadekar was out. So I got up and went to meet him. We had become good friends on the tour and I always called him 'Wadders' and he called me 'Johnners'. So it was with some confidence that I approached him and in front of the camera asked him:

'What happened, Wadders?' Instead of the smile I was expecting, I noticed that his face was completely blank. Thinking he had not heard me over the applause of the crowd I repeated the question. To my utter astonishment he said in broken English: 'Sorry—I no speak English. I do not understand,' and continued on his way to the pavilion. 'But Wadders,' I gasped, 'we've often talked together during the tour—surely you understand? How did you get out?' But it was no good. He brushed me aside murmuring: 'Me no speak English—sorry,' and disappeared into the pavilion.

Was my face red as I turned to face the camera! I tried to laugh it off—not very successfully—before I hurriedly handed over to the commentator.

I discovered afterwards that Wadekar had got permission from his Captain, the Nawab of Patandi, to pull my leg. I must admit that he succeeded in a big way!

In 1960 England won the first three Tests to beat South Africa 3–0 in the series and there was no real tension when we came to the Oval for the last Test. On the last morning play was particularly dull, with light rain falling and England batting drearily. In the television box we were becoming a bit bored, so we thought that we would liven things up a bit. We had one of those very rude seaside postcards and put it inside an envelope from one of the telegrams which we had received. We addressed it to Neil Adcock and persuaded the South African 12th man Griffin to take it out on to the field at the end of an over. He did so and Neil stuffed it into his pocket until he had bowled another over. He then opened the 'telegram', saw the postcard and burst out laughing. He signalled to the rest of his team to have a look and even the two umpires Charlie Elliott and

Eddie Phillipson could not resist taking a peep. Soon everyone on the field was laughing and all we said on TV was that Adcock had obviously had some very good news from home. We heard our colleagues in the radio box next to us speculating. Had Adcock's wife had twins or had he won the pools or what? At the lunch interval Neil had to make a statement in the press but though he now knew who had sent it, he didn't give us away, but admitted it was a practical joke. At any rate, it had cheered things up a bit!

In 1974 on the Saturday of the 2nd Test at Lord's v Pakistan it rained most of the day and there were constant

interruptions. We were doing our best to fill in with talk so that we did not have to return to the studio for music. At 2.30 p.m. we were all sitting in the box having a general discussion, when Henry Blofeld got stuck into some topic in which he was especially interested. When he gets excited Henry talks very fast and hardly draws breath. On this occasion he looked straight into the microphone and gabbled away at a great pace for about three or four minutes, completely ignoring the rest of us. We got a bit fed up, so all quietly left our seats and went out of the box. We then got Peter Baxter, our producer, to slip note in front of Henry as he was in full spate. The note simply read 'Keep going till 6.30 p.m.' It momentarily stopped

Henry in his tracks, as he looked round the box and saw that he was alone and had to keep talking by himself for at least four hours. But he carried on bravely and after a few minutes we had mercy on him, and slipped back into our seats . . .

In 1977 during a rainy session at the Oval Test Freddie Trueman asked us all in the box if we knew what was the fastest thing on two wheels in London. None of us did, so he enlightened us. 'An Arab riding a bicycle through Golders Green!'

During another rainy session I remembered a story someone told me during the luncheon interval. So I asked Trevor Bailey: 'What would you call a French circus artist who is shot out of a cannon?' Neither he nor anyone else in the box could think of the answer. So I told them: 'Napoleon Blownapart'.

As I have said, people are very kind and send all sorts of gifts to the commentary box—sweets, chocolates, biscuits—even wine. At Lord's in 1977 some kind lady sent me a gorgeous sticky chocolate cake. I cut it into slices and during a rather dull bit of play I noticed Alan MacGilvray standing chatting at the back of the box. So whilst commentating I turned round and offered him a piece of the cake, which he gratefully took. I saw him take a good mouthful and as soon as the next ball had been bowled I said, 'I'll now ask Alan MacGilvray what he thought of that particular delivery—Alan come up to the mike and give your opinion.' The result was hysterical. Alan tried desperately to speak and crumbs spattered all over the box. He managed to gulp down some of the cake and

spoke a few incoherent words. But by that time it didn't matter. Everyone in the box was laughing out loud.

Funnily enough Alan was concerned on another occasion where laughter in the box actually stopped us broadcasting for at least twenty seconds—a long time for silence on the air. It was at Edgbaston during the England v Australia Test Match in 1977. There was a long break in play due to a heavy thunderstorm, and as usual we were having our chat show in the box rather than return to the studio. We were discussing how cricket seemed to run in families. I quoted Penny Cowdrey, and said how she had helped her three sons by bowling to them in the garden. I went on to say that only the week before she had taken five wickets against the Junior Boys XI at her youngest son Graham's preparatory school at Broadstairs. I then added mischievously, 'Yes, they tell me that on that day her swingers were practically unplayable!'

As I suspected this remark started everyone in the box giggling. Under some difficulty we continued the discussion and mentioned Vic Richardson's daughter who for years bowled at her three sons Ian, Greg and Trevor Chappell. Don Mosey said that Trevor was having a wonderful season in the Lancashire League and that people were saying he was as good as Ian and Greg. 'Let's just check on that from someone who knows the Chappell family well,' I went on with confidence, knowing that Alan was sitting quietly at the back of the box. I turned round and saw that Alan was fast asleep, chin resting deep on his chest, with a slight whistling sound coming down his nose. This set us all off laughing again, but to cover up, and to save Alan any embarrassment, I managed to blurt out: 'I'm sorry, I'm afraid Alan must have left the box.' With that Alan woke with a snort and a start and said:

44

'What's going on? What do you want to know?' But by then we were too helpless with laughter to tell him. All the listeners could hear was a gentle hissing and sobbing as we tried to stem our laughter. Nobody could speak and Don Mosey who is the worst giggler of the lot and had started the whole thing off, managed to make a bolt for the door, leaving me to hold the fort. After a long silence which seemed ages but was probably only 20 seconds I managed to speak, and came clean with the listeners, and told them exactly what had happened.

Jokes in the Rain

Next we come to a sample of the jokes and puns with which we have regaled the poor listeners when Rain has stopped Play. Don't judge them too harshly! Remember they were made 'at a stroke'.

On one MCC tour of Australia, the team were travelling by train. A girl was nursing a baby in a carriage, the only other occupant of which was a man who kept staring at the baby. He couldn't take his eyes off it, and the girl became more and more embarrassed and annoyed. Finally she could stand it no longer and asked the man why he was staring so. He replied that he would rather not say. But when the girl persisted he said he was sorry but he was staring because the baby was the ugliest baby he had ever seen in his life. This naturally upset the girl who broke into floods of tears and taking the baby went and stood in the corridor.

She was still crying when the MCC team came along the corridor on their way to the restaurant car. They all passed her except one of the players, who being a decent chap, stopped to ask her why she was crying. She told him that she had just been insulted by a man in her carriage. So he said: 'Well, cheer up. I'll bring you back a cup of tea from the restuarant car. That should make you feel better.' So off he went and returned in about five minutes. 'Here's your cup of tea,' he said to the girl, 'and what's more I've also brought a banana for the monkey!' What happened then is not related!

My favourite cricket story occurred at the Duke of Norfolk's lovely ground at Arundel. His team were playing the Sussex Martlets but just before the start they found they

had only one umpire. The Duke said he would go and get his butler Meadows who was cleaning the silver down at the Castle. He did not know much about cricket but would be better than nothing. So Meadows was fetched, put into a white coat and the game began with the Duke's side batting. They did not do too well and with seven wickets down the Duke himself came into bat. He was at the non-strikers' end and Meadows was standing at square leg. The batsman thought he had better give the Duke the strike, so pushed the ball to cover and called 'Come on, your Grace.'

Unfortunately the Duke slipped and landed flat on his face in the middle of the pitch. Cover point threw the ball over the top of the stumps to the wicket-keeper who whipped off the bails with the Duke yards short of the crease. 'How's that?' everyone roared, and looked at Meadows at square leg. There was a pregnant silence. What would he do? Would he give his master out? After a second or two's pause Meadows drew himself up to his full height and with his two hands in front of his chest in a way butlers have, he gave his verdict: 'His Grace is not in!'

A southerner who was staying in Leeds decided to watch the annual Roses Match between Yorkshire and Lancashire. Before the game started he found a seat and went off to get a drink—placing his hat neatly on the seat where he had been sitting. On returning a few minutes later he found that his hat had been removed to the floor, and a large Yorkshireman was sitting on his seat. Somewhat diffidently he said, 'Excuse me, Sir, I think you are sitting on my seat, I reserved it with my hat.' The Yorkshireman replied, 'I'm sorry, lad, it's bums what keep seats up 'ere, not 'ats.'

'SANDWICHES! WHAT BLOODY CHEESE SANDWICHES?'

Before the start of a needle village match, the home Captain found he was one short. In desperation he was looking round the ground for someone he could rope in to play when he spotted an old horse grazing quietly in the field next door. So he went up to him and asked him if he would like to make up the side. The horse stopped eating and said: 'Well, I haven't played for some time and am a bit out of practice but if you're pushed, I'll certainly help you out,' and so saying jumped over the fence and sat down in a deck-chair in front of the pavilion. The visitors lost the toss and the home side batted first, the horse being put in last. They were soon 23 for 9 and the horse made his way to the wicket wearing those sort of leather shoes horses have on when they are pulling a roller or a mower. He soon showed his eye was well in and hit the bowling all over the field. When he wasn't hitting sixes he was galloping for quick singles and never once said 'Neigh' when his partner called him for a run. Finally he was out hoof before wicket for a brilliant 68, and the home side had made 99.

When the visitors batted the home Captain put the horse in the deep and he saved many runs by galloping round the boundary and hoofing the ball back to the wicket-keeper. However the visitors were not losing any wickets and were soon 50 for 0. The home Captain had tried all his regular bowlers in vain when he suddenly thought of the horse. He had batted brilliantly and now was fielding better than anyone. At least he could do no worse than the other bowlers. So he called out to him: 'Horse, would you like to take the next over at the vicarage end?' The horse looked surprised, 'Of course I wouldn't,' he replied. 'Whoever heard of a horse who could BOWL!'

In a Middlesex match at Lord's before the war Walter Robins had just completed a very productive over as far as the batsmen were concerned, and decided that it was time to make a change. He called over to a Middlesex fast bowler, 'Take the next over at this end, Jim.' Umpire Bill Reeves walked across to the retiring Robins and said, 'Do you want your sweater, Sir?' As it was a hot and perspiring day, Robins rather grumpily said to Reeves, 'Keep the b . . . . sweater; and you know what you can do with it.'

'What, Sir?' said Reeves, 'swords and all!'

A man, whose wife was in hospital expecting a baby, telephoned one afternoon to see what the news was. By mistake he got the local cricket ground. When he asked what was the latest position the reply came back, 'There are seven out already, and the last two were ducks!'

And finally what about the unorthodox batsman who, like Brian Close, could play equally well either right- or left-handed. His opponents never knew which it would be until he took up his stance at the crease. One of them asked him how he decided which way he would play. He replied that if, when he woke up in the morning, his wife was lying on her right side, then he would bat right-handed. If she was lying on her left side, then he batted left-handed. 'But what happens if she is lying on her back?' asked the opponent. 'In that case,' said the man, 'I ring up the club to say I will be an hour late!'

'HE ALSO LIKES A BACON SANDWICH AT EXACTLY 11·52!'

Batting

Lastly the stories which have been told to fill in time when Rain Stops Play. We all have our special favourites among the great characters which cricket has always produced. I suspect that John Arlott's favourites are George Gunn, Bomber Wells or anyone from Hampshire. My own is certainly the one and only Patsy Hendren. Everyone's favourite seems to be Freddie Trueman himself. I hope that you will find yours among this sample of stories which have been told in the Box.

Dr W. G. Grace had just packed his bag one morning and was ready to go off to play for Gloucestershire, when a lady rushed up to his door and said: 'Can you come quickly, Doctor, I think my twins have got the measles': 'I'm sorry, Ma'am, but I am just going off to Gloucester to play cricket and can't stop. But contact me at the ground if their temperatures reach 210 for two.'

George Gunn, when playing for Nottinghamshire against Glamorgan, started to walk off the field at half-past one with the impression that it was time for lunch. However, under the conditions for that match, lunch was not due to be taken until 2.00 p.m. and Gunn was recalled to continue his innings; he lifted his bat away from the next ball—was comprehensibly bowled—making no attempt to play the ball—and as he retired to the pavilion, said 'You can have your lunch, gentlemen, when you like, but I always take mine at 1.30 p.m.'

During Len Hutton's tour of Australia, Frank Tyson's tremendous speed caused dismay and destruction amongst batsmen wherever he bowled. On one occasion when he was at his fastest, he had run through a side until it was the turn of the number eleven batsman to come in. Looking pale and apprehensive he came down the pavilion steps, but was so nervous that he couldn't close the catch of the pavilion gate. A voice from the crowd shouted: 'Leave it open, you won't be long!'

A batsman had played and missed a number of times. Yabba, the famous Sydney Hill barracker, shouted out to the bowler: 'Send him down a grand piano, and see if he can play *that*!'

In a match against Gloucestershire, Brian Close was fielding at forward short leg with Freddie Trueman bowling. Martin Young received a short ball which he hit right in the middle of the bat. It hit Close on the right side of the head and rebounded to first slip who caught it!

Close seemed none the worse but when he returned to the pavilion at the next interval a member asked him: 'That was a terrible blow; aren't you worried standing so near? What *would* have happened if the ball had hit you slap between the eyes?'

'He'd have been caught at cover,' replied the indomitable Yorkshire captain!

When 'Bomber' Wells came in to bat for Nottinghamshire

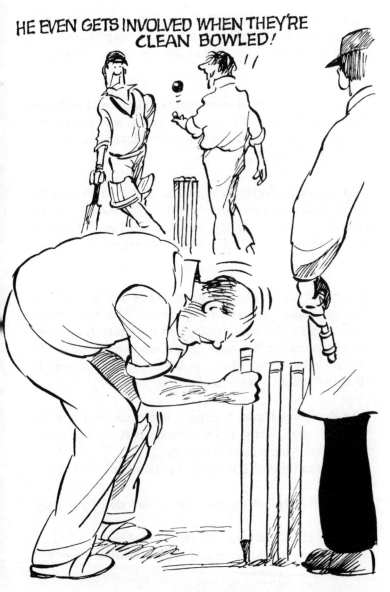

against the Australians at Trent Bridge in 1964, Neil Hawke was in devastating form. The umpire, ready to give him guard, said: 'What do you want, Bomber?': 'Help!'

Arthur Wood, to a batsman who had played and missed at three successive balls, each of which just grazed the stumps without disturbing the bails: 'Have you ever tried walking on water?'

And to Hedley Verity at Bramall Lane in 1935, after H. B. Cameron had just hit Verity for thirty in one over Wood offered this advice: 'Keep 'em there Hedley. Thou hast him in two minds—he don't know whether t'smack thee for four or six.'

It appears that when 'Bomber' Wells was playing for Gloucestershire he was batting one day with Sam Cook.

They got into a terrible tangle over a short single, with Sam just making the crease by hurling himself flat on the ground. As he lay there panting he shouted out to 'Bomber': 'Call!'—and 'Bomber' shouted back: 'Tails!'

The Reverend David Sheppard was embroiled one day with 'Bomber' Wells, and with edges past slip and short-leg was enjoying a good deal of luck.

'I should think, Vicar,' said the 'Bomber', 'that you've been on your praying mat.'

'Indeed,' replied the Reverend. 'But don't *you* pray, Brian?'

'No, I always rely on skill and a bit of luck.'

'Well,' said the Reverend, 'which is showing the greater profit at the moment?'

57

Alf Gover, Surrey and England, as a young 19 year old, arrived at Lord's for his first Middlesex v Surrey match. When he got to the old 'Pro's' dressing room, only one other person was there—the great Patsy Hendren. 'Hello, young chap,' he called out, 'what's your name?'

'Alf Gover, Sir.'

'What do you do?'

'I bowl.'

'Quick?' said Patsy.

'Very quick,' he answered proudly. Patsy looked round the room to make sure that he was not overheard, came over to him and said, very confidentially: 'Look son, I don't mind quick bowling, you can push it down at me as fast as you like, only—' another conspiratorial glance round—'only I don't like 'em if they are pitched short. You know this is my home ground and they like me to get a few. My peepers aren't as good as they were and I can't pick up the ball as fast as I used to, so keep them well up to me, won't you?' Alf pondered on this self-admitted fear of the great England and Middlesex batsman and decided that there was a great chance for him to make his name.

He happened to be bowling from the pavilion end when Patsy came in, and said to himself: 'Ah, here's that old man who can't see and doesn't like short-pitched balls—so here goes.' His first ball to him was very short, just outside the leg stump and as fast as he could bowl it. It was promptly hooked for six into the Tavern. 'Fluke,' he said to himself and sent him down a similar short ball, only this time on the middle stump. Patsy took two steps back and cut it for four past third man. 'I've got him scared now—he's running away,' he said to himself as he walked back to his mark. Down came his third ball just the same as the other two and it went sailing away for six into the

Mound Stand. At the end of the over Jack Hobbs went across to him from cover. 'What are you bowling short at Mr Hendren for, son?'

'He's afraid of them,' Alf replied.

The 'Master' stared in amazement. 'Who told you that?' he asked.

'He did, Mr Hobbs,' said Alf.

'Young man. Never do it again', said Hobbs. 'Patsy is still the best hooker of fast bowling in the world. May I remind you that he's an Irishman, and every night he kisses the Blarney Stone!'

On another occasion after suffering from a surfeit of dropped catches in the slips off his bowling, Alf Gover, was

having a drink with some of the offenders after close of play. After a while one of them said: 'Well, so long Alf, I must be off. I've got a train to catch.' Alf replied: 'So long. Hope you have better luck—with the train!'

Patsy Hendren was fond of telling this apocryphal (I hope!) story. Once when travelling in a train on his way to a match he sat opposite an ashen-faced stranger, who had his coat collar turned up around his ears. He looked so ill and thoroughly miserable that Patsy was moved to ask him what the trouble was. In a hoarse whisper—hardly able to speak—the man confided that he was a very keen cricketer, but had recently let his side down badly by making five ducks in a row. Said Patsy: 'Oh dear, oh dear, if I ever made five ducks in a row I would cut my throat.'

The Stranger (in a whisper): 'I have.'

On one occasion he was fielding on the boundary by the famous Hill on the Sydney Cricket Ground. The batsman hit the ball high in the air towards him. As it soared higher and higher into the air a raucous voice from the Hill shouted, 'Patsy, if you miss the catch you can sleep with my sister.'

Later Patsy was asked what he had done. 'Oh', he replied, 'as I hadn't seen his sister, I caught the ball.'

Just before he retired he was batting against Derbyshire on a wet pitch that was slippery with mud. Walter Robins was his partner and was batting against the leg breaks of T. B. Mitchell. Robins who always used his feet to attack slow bowlers, had got into the habit of dancing down the pitch and if he missed the ball, walking straight on to the pavilion without looking round at the wicket-keeper. Mitchell was bowling from the pavilion end and as usual

Robins danced down the pitch, missed the ball and continued walking towards the pavilion without so much as a backward glance. Patsy immediately shouted 'He's missed it'—so Robins turned quickly round and flung himself on the ground bat stretched out towards the stumps. There was a roar of laughter from the players and the crowd, as Robins slowly got up, shirt, flannels and pads covered in mud. He looked up to see the bails lying on the ground and Harry Elliott the wicket-keeper chatting to the slip, having obviously brought off a neat stumping! When Patsy was asked how Robins had taken it he said that he hadn't been too pleased! Knowing R.W.V.R. that was putting it mildly.

Leicestershire were playing Nottinghamshire and Harold Larwood was bowling at his fastest and was in his most frightening mood. The light was very bad and he had taken four quick wickets when it was Alec Skelding's turn to bat. He came down the pavilion steps very slowly, then groped his way along the railings in front of the pavilion, shouting to the members, 'Can anyone tell me where this match is being played . . . ?'

A similar story is told about Jack Newman when he came out to bat with Lord Tennyson, and his Lordship called down the wicket to Newman, 'Why don't you appeal against the light, Jack? They won't listen to me.'
To which Newman replied, 'I can hear you, my Lord, but I can't see you . . . where are you?'

On 1 January 1925, Hobbs and Sutcliffe of Yorkshire and England batted all day against Australia in Melbourne, putting on 283 for the opening partnership, in reply to what was then a record Test total of 600 runs by Australia. There were 75,000 people on the ground, and as the day wore on they began to barrack their team more and more. (It is worth remembering perhaps that the bowlers included Jack Gregory, Charlie Kelleway, Arthur Mailey and Arthur Richardson.) But the barrackers were merciless on them, 'You'll never get 'em out—you'll have to

63

LEFT ARM ENEMAS
OVER THE WICKET...

burn 'em out—send for the Fire Brigade, they'll get 'em out—put the roller on—put the clock on—etc., etc.' But the culminating point of the whole day's batting came between the tea interval and the close of play. There was a momentary silence which was broken by a terrific raucous voice which yelled out, 'Send for Nurse Blank, she'll get the b . . . . s out!'

(Nurse Blank was a well-known midwife who shortly before the Test Match had made the headlines in an abortion case!)

In 1958 at Bridgetown against the West Indies Hanif Mohammad, Pakistan was playing his marathon innings of 337 which lasted for 16 hours 13 minutes. A West

Indian supporter, perched perilously on a branch of a tree, stuck it for most of the day but then falling asleep either from the heat or boredom (!) fell with a resounding crash to the ground and knocked himself out. He was taken off to hospital where he was unconscious for some time. When he eventually came round one of the hospital nurses told him he'd been 'out' for two hours. Quick as a flash he exclaimed: 'I only hope Hanif has been too.'

Bowling and Fielding

Arthur Mailey was bowling for New South Wales in the famous match in which Victoria scored 1,107 against them. Mailey's figures were 4 for 362. He said afterwards, 'I should have had an even better analysis if a bloke in a brown trilby hat sitting in the sixth row of the pavilion roof hadn't dropped two sitters!'

Harold Larwood was once staying with a friend in the West Country, and visited a village cricket match on the Saturday afternoon. The visiting side were one short and Larwood was pressed to play without anyone knowing who he was. As both umpires came from the home side, who were batting, it proved difficult to get them out. In desperation the Captain asked Larwood if he could bowl. He said that he would have a try and, taking a short run, sent down an off-spinner, which the batsman missed. It hit him in the middle of both legs which were right in front of the wicket. To the appeal—'Not out' was the reply. The next one, a leg break, was snicked into the wicket-keeper's hands. Again 'Not out' was the reply. Larwood then took his usual run of over 20 yards and sent down a thunderbolt which knocked all three stumps out of the ground. Turning to the umpire he said, 'We very nearly had him that time, didn't we?'

Joe Hardstaff said of Roly Thompson of Warwickshire who used to take an unnecessarily long run: 'He takes such a long run that you're out of form by the time he reaches the stumps.'

In 1937, against Yorkshire, Fred Price, the Middlesex wicket-keeper, caught seven catches in an innings—a record at that time. He was having a drink in the Tavern after the game, when a lady came up to him and said, 'Oh, Mr Price, I did admire your wicket-keeping today. I was so excited, I nearly fell off the balcony.'

'If you had done so, madam,' he replied, 'on today's form I would have caught you too!'

HARDLY A DOLLY!

Whilst in Australia with the 1962/3 MCC team poor David Sheppard came in for more than his fair share of dropped catches. The story was going around that a young English couple who had settled in Australia were due to have their first-born christened. The husband suggested that it

THAT'S 6 OUT OF 10...SHALL WE
TAKE A CHANCE?

would be nice if they got David Sheppard to do it for them. 'Oh no,' said the horrified wife, 'not likely, he would only drop it!'

At Cheltenham when Surrey were playing Gloucestershire, Gover was asked by umpire Bill Reeves whether he wanted guard: 'No, thanks, I've played here before.'

Godfrey Evans, Kent and England, made a particularly good stumping on the leg-side when playing in an up-country match on one of his tours of Australia. As he whipped off the bails he shouted to the umpire, 'How's that?', and the umpire replied, 'Bloody marvellous!'

Cecil Parkin once suggested to his captain, Johnny Douglas, whose bowling figures were nought for plenty on the score–board, yet still kept himself on, 'Why not go on at t'other end: maybe tha'll see score board better from there.'

E. J. (Tiger) Smith said once 'I never missed a catch in my life. They just dropped out!'

During an MCC tour of India, under the Captaincy of Lionel Tennyson, half the team were down with dysentery. Alf Gover had to leave his sick-bed to make up the eleven for a match. Ian Peebles, in his own inimitable way, has described what happened then. Alf's first few overs were uneventful, but during the third, only the most acute observer would have been alarmed at the tense expression on his face as he started on his long, hustling run. It was when he shot past the crouching umpire and thundered down the pitch with the undelivered ball in his hand that it became obvious that something was amiss. The batsman, fearing a personal assault, sprang smartly backward, but the flannelled giant sped past looking neither to right nor left. Past wicketkeeper, slips and fine leg in a flash, he hurtled up the pavilion steps in a cloud of dusty gravel and was gone. That he has never received full credit for this record is due to the lack of timing apparatus and the distance, from the start of his run to his uncomfortable destination, not being a recognised one.

As, in the tight-lipped precipitation of his flight, he had been unable to give any hint of his future movements, fine leg, after a moment's thought, followed up the steps and rescued the ball from the bowler's convulsive grasp.

It was a Sunday in Australia, and Percy Chapman and Patsy Hendren decided to get away from it all and borrowed a car for a run into the country. After a few miles they went round a corner and saw a cricket match about to start in a field adjoining the road. As all cricketers are wont to do—they stopped the car with the intention of watching the game for a few minutes. The car no sooner stopped than an Australian strolled over to the car and said, 'Do either of you chaps play cricket?'

Chapman pointed to Patsy and said, 'He plays a little.'

'Good Oh,' said the fellow, 'we are a man short; will you make up for us?'

Although it was Patsy's day off he obliged, and as his adopted side were fielding the captain sent him out to long-on. Patsy went to the allotted position, and as the field was on a slope he was out of sight of the pitch. He had nothing to do except throw the ball in occasionally. He was lost to sight for a long time when at last a towering hit was sent in his direction. Patsy caught the ball and ran up the hill shouting, 'I caught it, I caught it.' The batsman looked at him with daggers drawn—it was *his* captain. 'You lunatic—*they* were out twenty minutes ago. *We* are batting now!'

Each year at the beginning of the season, Yorkshire used to play some one-day matches against clubs around the county. The idea was to give the team some practice out in the middle before starting their championship matches. One year they were playing against a club just outside York. Yorkshire fielded first and Freddie Trueman soon got among the wickets, bowling with surprising speed and ferocity for so early in the season. He had taken the first five wickets and the next batsman emerged from the pavi-

lion. He was an upright military figure, with bristling white moustache and an old-fashioned I Zingari cap on his head, complete with button on the top. The sleeves of his cream shirt were buttoned down to the wrist and he had on a pair of those skeleton pads which used to be fashionable in the days of W.G. He was an imposing figure, but understandably enough he looked a trifle apprehensive at what he had to face.

Norman Yardley, the Yorkshire captain, saw him coming and, realising the county were doing a bit too well, went up to Freddie and said: 'This is Brigadier X. He is an important member of the county. Let him get a few.' So Freddie, in his most affable and friendly manner, went up to the Brigadier as he approached the wicket and said: 'Good morning, Brigadier, don't worry. With my first ball I'll give you one to get off the mark.' The Brigadier looked greatly relieved, but his expression changed as Freddie went on: 'Aye, and with my second I'll pin thee against flippin' sightscreen!'

In a Lancashire match a fast bowler was bowling on a bad wicket, and the opening batsman—who shall be nameless—had to face a number of terrifying deliveries. The first whizzed past his left ear—the second nearly knocked his cap off—and the third struck him an awful blow over the heart. He collapsed and lay on the ground—then after a minute or two got up and prepared to take strike again. The umpire asked him if he was ready—he replied, 'Yes, but I would like the sightscreen moved.'

'Certainly,' said the umpire. 'Where would you like it?'

The batsman replied, 'About half way down the wicket between me and the bowler!'

Yorkshire were playing Somerset in the good old days.

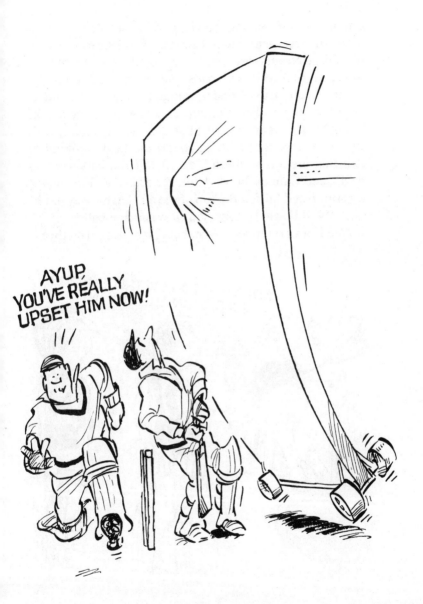

Emmott Robinson was bowling when in came the next batsman; a real gentleman, I Zingari, bristling moustache, silk shirt ('Never wore a vest in my life!'), spotless batting trousers, well-whitened pads and boots, and a highly-coloured fancy cap. 'Good morning, Robinson,' he said on his way to the wicket. Emmott took an immediate dislike to him. The batsman arrived at the wicket, took guard, and then took ages looking round the field, walking or strutting around as he did so. At last the batsman was ready, and Emmott bowled him a snorter, pitching on the leg stump and hitting the top of the off. On his way out he said, 'Well bowled, Robinson, it was a fine ball.'

And Emmott replied, 'Aye, but t'were wasted on thee.'

'...NOT A BAD FOLLOW THROUGH FOR AN OLD 'UN ALL THE SAME!'

Just before he retired Tom Graveney was sweeping the leaves away from the door of his house in Winchcombe. Two boys passed him on their bikes and he heard the following conversation: 'I say, I think Tom Graveney lives somewhere here'—'Yes, he does, in that house where the old man is sweeping the leaves.'

Umpires

Ray Robinson tells of the occasion when umpire George Borwick was signalling to an attendant who was moving the sightscreen at the batsman's request. Borwick was holding his arm aloft for quite a long time as a signal to the attendant to keep on pushing. Yabba, the famous Sydney barracker, noticed the upstretched arm and shouted: 'It's no use, umpire, you can't leave the ground—you'll have to wait till the lunch interval, like the rest of us!'

An umpire (who shall be nameless) after Johnny Wardle enquired: 'You know, I think that ball would have hit the wicket. Where do you think it would have hit?': 'How should I know—the gentleman's leg was in the way!'

Charlie Knott of Hampshire was bowling to Dusty Rhodes of Derbyshire and roared out a terrific appeal for a catch at the wicket. 'Howizee?' Alec Skelding: 'Oh, he's not at all well and was even worse last night.'

Skelding after an appeal for a run-out which was a very close thing: 'Gentlemen—it's a photo finish—and I haven't got time to develop the photo. NOT OUT.'

When Harold Larwood played against Wilfred Rhodes for the first time he noticed that the Yorkshire batsman when taking his stance had the front of his left foot cocked off the ground. 'What's he doing that for?' said Lol to umpire Bill Reeves.

'Oh, he always stands like that,' said Bill.

'He won't to me,' said Larwood, and rushing up to the wicket bowled a full toss which landed with a mighty crack on Rhodes' toes. 'How's that?' yelled Larwood.

'Bloody painful I should think,' said Reeves.

Alec Skelding was umpiring a match on a hot, dusty day. One of the bowlers had a full set of false teeth, and as he

ran up to deliver a particularly fast ball all his teeth fell out on to the ground. The ball hit the batsman on the pad and the bowler turned round and mouthed unintelligible noises. Alec, quick to see what had happened, said 'I beg your pardon. I cannot tell what you say.' The bowler tried again but Alec still pretended he could not decipher his words. So the bowler stooped down, recovered his dentures covered in dust, replaced them and turning round said rather grittily: 'How's that?'

'Not out!'

Surrey were playing Middlesex at the Oval and Bill Reeves was one of the umpires. Nigel Haig opened the bowling and Andrew Sandham went in first for Surrey. Not being very tall a ball from Haig hit him in the navel and there was a loud appeal. 'Not out,' said Reeves. 'Why not?' asked Haig. 'Too high,' said Reeves. Haig went back to his mark muttering, possibly thinking that even if a ball hit a little chap like him on the head it couldn't be too high. A few balls later a beautiful ball beat him all ends up and hit Sandham on the pads. 'What about that one then?' yelled Haig. 'Not out,' said Reeves. 'Why not?' said Haig. 'Too low!' said Reeves—and that ended all arguments for that day!

When he was at school Gilbert Harding hated cricket. The headmaster, appreciating this, excused him playing on condition that he took some other exercise such as walking or tennis. But the games master was always very annoyed about this and got his own back one day (so he thought) by making Gilbert Harding umpire in the annual match of the Masters v the Boys. The Masters batted first and the games master, resplendent in his Oxford Authentic cap, batted superbly and was 99 not out when a bowler from the end at which Gilbert Harding was umpiring hit him high up on the left thigh. 'How's that?' said the bowler.

'Out,' said Gilbert. The games master was furious and as he passed Gilbert on his way back to the pavilion said, 'Harding, you weren't paying attention. I wasn't out.'

Gilbert replied, 'On the contrary, sir, I *was* paying attention and you weren't out!'

In a village match a visiting batsman was hit high on the chest by the local fast bowler—the village blacksmith.

To his surprise the bowler appealed for lbw, and to his even greater surprise the umpire gave him out. As he

passed the umpire on his way back to the pavilion, the batsman said, 'I couldn't possibly have been out, it hit me in the chest.'

'Well,' said the umpire, 'you look in the local *Gazette* next Thursday, and you'll see you were out right enough.'

'*You* look,' snorted the batsman, 'I am the Editor!'

In a Central Lancashire League match a batsman snicked the ball hard on to his pads, from where it went down towards long leg. He ran one run, but was amazed on approaching the other end, to hear the bowler appealing for lbw. To his horror the umpire then put his finger up. Unable to contain himself the batsman blurted out, 'I can't be out lbw I hit it.' 'I know you did,' said the umpire. 'I'm only signalling byes.'

In a village cricket match a very fat batsman came in to bat, and as he was taking up his stance at the wicket the local umpire confided to the visiting bowler: 'We have a special rule for him. If you hit him in front it's lbw, if you hit him behind it's a wide!'

W. G. Grace was batting on a very windy day, and a fast bowler succeeded in getting one past him which just flicked the bails off. The Doctor stood his ground and said to the umpire, 'Windy day today, umpire.'

Whereupon the umpire replied, 'Very windy indeed, Doctor—mind it doesn't blow your cap off on the way back to the pavilion!'